This Book

This book was written to explain how to use Conitec's 3D Gamestudio.

For more information visit **http://www.create3dgames.com**

Copyright

Trademarks

Disclaimer

Table of Contents

Chapter 1 - Introduction

Before you start:

Download - 3dGamestuio software from **Conitec 3dGamestudio**
http://www.3dgamestudio.com

Download - **lite-C software**. http://www.3dgamestudio.com/

Download - **Paint.net**. Paint.net is a free image and photo editing software. There is an active online community involved with Paint.net. http://www.getpaint.net

3D Gamestudio Software

* The **Extra Edition** is the basic game development system.

* The **Commercial Edition** adds network and shader features.

* The **Pro Edition** includes a file packer/encrypter and 12 months email support."
Conitec November 2009

"**Gamestudio/A7** is 100% compatible to it's predecessor, Gamestudio/A6 version 6.60. The A6 templates and the A5 templates still run under A7. The A7 engine renders much faster than A6 and contains hundreds of new features, such as direct access to all DirectX functions, a full physics engine in all editions, an ABT scene manager, improved multiplayer functions, improved terrain renderer, radiosity light mapper, atlas mapping, unlimited dynamic lights, decal system, shader viewer and shader library." *Conitec January 2010*

GameStudio's MED is used to create the models for
3D Game Studio.

Atari light-C Script Editor
"The lite-C package contains a complete development environment with 3D model and terrain editor, code editor, compiler, debugger, an integrated 3D engine, a physics engine, many samples including DirectX and OpenGL programs, and a tutorial with 24 easy workshops." *Conitec January 2010*

Gamestudio World Editor

The **World Editor**, WED is Gamestudio's main editor. WED is where the editor creates the Virtual World or level. Users can create games by designing their own environments and creating and importing models. The software allows users to add textures, create scripts, designs, give models attributes and actions, add sound, add properties such as fluidity and create and add backgrounds.

 The World Editor - WED is the location where users merge all the components.

Users of Gamestudio can **import file formats** from other computer games such as Quake. Pre-constructed **levels** (MAP files), **textures** (WAD files) and **3D models** (MDL or 3D files) can be imported into Gamestudio.

What's in This Book

This book is for beginners who are new to Conitec's Gamestudio software. The book is written as a visual guide for understanding how Gamestudio's WED World Level Editor works. The book is filled with lessons and screen shots to "show" the reader how to use Conitec's 3dGamestudio software. Not every menu item will be covered. This book is for a new user who wants to master the basics right away and get started as quickly as possible. A book this size cannot possibly cover anything more then the "getting started" lessons.

The book will start with the absolute basics of adding a cube, hollowing it and starting the process of creating a room. Texturing is explained and how to use Paint.net, a free software program, to create custom textures. Primitives are explained. Instructions are included on how to use three of Gamestudio's basic primitives to create and texture a lamp. The last section explains entities. Follow the steps to add a human player and a computer player to a basic shooter game. The models (players) used in the book are models which have been downloaded from Gamestudio's website. Instructions for downloading the models are included in this book.

This book is designed to be followed from beginning to end. Each chapter presents information needed for the next chapter.

This is a Step-by-Step Instruction book which introduces the basics and shows the reader how to use the software.

Chapter 2 - Getting Started

Open the WED Software

1. **Click** on **FILE** on the menu bar and select ➜ **NEW LEVEL**

   Info. **Or**, commands can also be accessed under MODE on the toolbar.

Add a Cube – Make a Room

Fig. 2-1

1   **Click on OBJECT ➜ ADD CUBE ➜ LARGE on the menu bar.**

   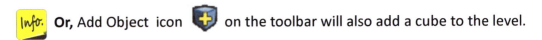
   Info. **Or,** Add Object icon ⬛ on the toolbar will also add a cube to the level.

2   **Click** ⬛ **SCALE** and use the arrows to re-size the cube.

3   **Moving the Objects** ⬛ – use the three arrows to position the box on the grid. The cube moves along X, Y and Z planes. Refer to Chapter 4, Primitives- for a more detailed explanation of positioning 3D objects in space.

This cube will be hollowed out to create a room. Selecting a solid cube to start this project will create thinner walls on the cube we hollow. Selecting the Gamestudio's existing hollow cubes from the menu creates a cube with thicker sides. It is more difficult to cut openings in thicker walls to pass through to other areas.

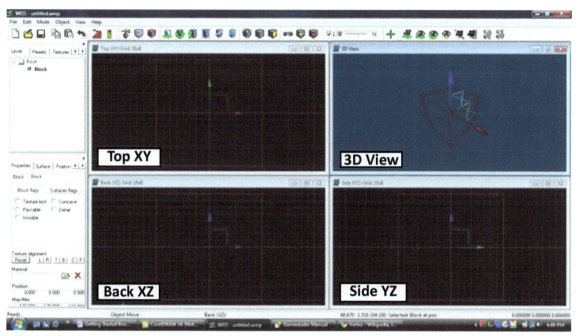

Fig. 2-2

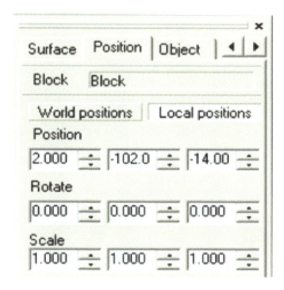

The **Top** (XY)Grid represents a view looking down into the top of the cube.
The Back view (XZ)
The Side (YZ)

Precise Placement of a Cube

On the local **Positions Tab** use the increase/decrease buttons to move the cube on the grid with precise accuracy.

Fig. 2-3

Making the Cube Hollow

1. **Click EDIT ➔ HOLLOW BLOCK** on the menu bar. Instead of a single line defining the cube you will now have double lines on all edges.

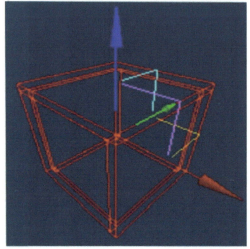

NOTE: Figure 2-4 is viewed in the WIRE View. On the toolbar, under <u>View</u> the cube can be changed to; WIRE, SOLID, or TEXTURED

Fig. 2-4

Level Tab

The Level Tab shows the tree of the current entities and objects in that level. **A cube is a block** (Fig. 2-5). **When you hollow the Block it becomes a Group** with blocks listed under it in the Level tree (Fig. 2-6) .

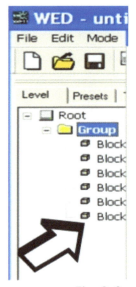

Cube Not hollowed (Block)   Fig. 2-5

Fig. 2-6

 Later, when an opening is created between cubes (rooms) it will be important to use a block (unhallowed cube) to create the opening.

Cube Hollowed
(Group with Blocks)

Add Position

Fig. 2-7

Click OBJECT → ADD POSITION on the menu bar to preview the room (Figure 2-7). Figure 2-8 shows the position after it is added.

Position is represented as a red camera inside the cube. You may move the camera in the room. Be sure the camera stays inside the walls of the room in all the grid views. After you build and run the level you are viewing the room through this camera "position."

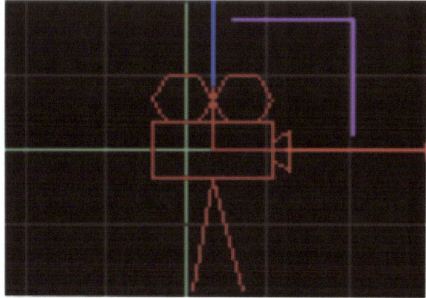

Position

Fig. 2-8

Add Lights

Click OBJECT ➔ ADD LIGHT

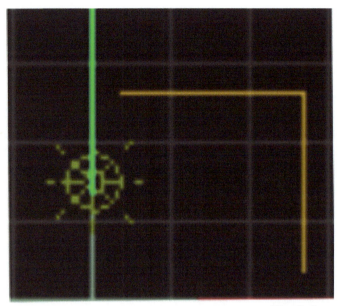

Light is represented as a circle with rays. The normal default lighting is dim. Multiple lights may be positioned around the room. Use light to feature walkways or light doorways. Lighting creates the atmosphere in the areas. You may use the default lighting throughout the entire project. You may add lighting as you build or add the lighting at the end of the project. **Position the light inside the room in the four views.**

Fig. 2-9

Save the File

Click FILE ➔ SAVE AS. Select the location where you want to save the file and name the file. **Click SAVE.** (At first saving work in the "work" folder is suggested.) Do not include spaces in the file name.

Build the Level

Click **BUILD. Click YES** to replace with **default texture**.

Build converts the map into the .WMB format, adds lighting information and generates the BSP tree, Binary Space Partitioning Tree.

Fig. 2-10

Map Compiler

Select lower visibility/light calculations to speed up the time needed to compile the level when you have a large level to compile

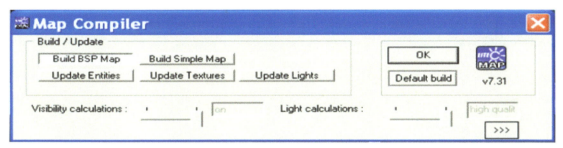

Fig. 2-11

Make adjustments on the Map Compiler. Click OK. (No adjustments will be needed in this example) Close first map compiler box. Level will automatically compile. Fig. 2-11

Click OK to close Map Compiler Generator.

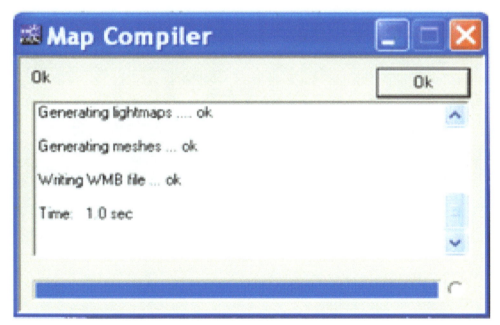

Fig. 2-12

Run the Level

Click **RUN level.**

After the program runs, the created room appears in a separate window. You are looking at the room through the camera "position". Fig. 2-13 If an error occurs refer to page 47 "Problems". Always check your file name for spaces or errors.

Moving Around the Room

Fig. 2-13

1   Use the **ARROW KEYS** to rotate around the room, side to side, zoom in and out.

2   **Hold down the RIGHT MOUSE BUTTON** to move the camera and view the different areas of the room.

    The room has one light in the center of the room. After viewing the room close the box and prepare to add an additional room.

Centering Your Work on the Screen

While working on your project, sometimes the cubes on the screen move off to the side and out of the Grid viewing area. Bring the cubes back to the center of your Grid screen by **Clicking on VIEW ➜ GOTO CENTER**. (Centers views to object scope)

 Or, **HOLD DOWN the RIGHT MOUSE BUTTON and drag the screen around till you center the image**, Or **Press the HOME key**.

Adding a Second Cube – Creating Additional Rooms

1 **Click OBJECT ➜ ADD CUBE ➜ MEDIUM** on the menu bar

  Or, **Add Object** icon on the toolbar will also add a cube to the level.

2 **With the New Cube Highlighted, Click on** **SCALE and pull the arrows to re-size the New Cube.**

3 **EDIT ➜ HOLLOW BLOCK** This hollows the cube into an open room.

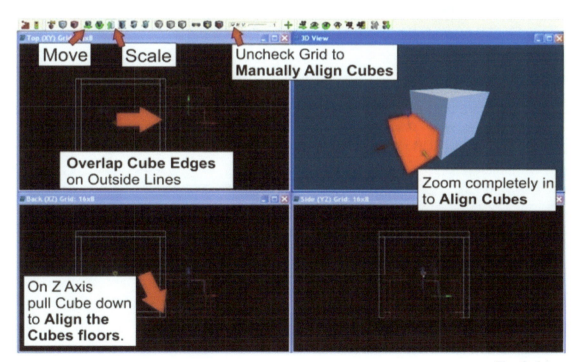

Fig. 2-14

Adding a Second Cube – Creating Additional Rooms - continued

3   **Click Move**   On the Top (XY) Grid, position your curser over the Red Arrow in the New cube and pull the New Cube over to the outside of the First Cube. Line up the edge of the New Cube with the "Outside line" of the First Cube. Adjust the New cube next to the First Cube. **Zoom all the way in** to see the adjoining edges of the rooms. If the rooms don't touch, modify the grid. (Refer to Fig. 2-14)

> **Info.**   **OPTIONAL – Modify Grid Scale for tight fit –**

Click on  **GRID SCALE. Slide the scale** back to a smaller number which will allow you to position the cubes closer. If the cube's lines still don't overlap then uncheck the slider and manually position the cubes. The rooms have to touch to place a doorway between them. If you have unchecked the grid slider re-check the grid slider box to turn the grid back on. Pull the slider to approximately 2 or 4. (Refer to the top of Fig. 2-14)

4   **Bottom Back (XZ) Grid, Click Move**   pull the New Cube down to line up the floors of the two cubes (rooms). (Refer to Fig. 2-14)

5   **FILE ➔ SAVE the Level ➔ Click on BUILD**   **➔ Click YES** to replace with default texture **➔ Click OK** on Map Compiler **➔ Click OK** to close Map Compiler **➔ Click**   **RUN ➔ Click OK** on Run Level.

Level Tab

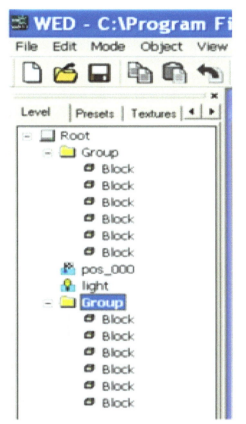

The completed rooms are shown on the Level Tab.

- The first room was added - GROUP with blocks.

- The Position (Camera) was added.

- The Light was added.

- The second room was added – GROUP with blocks.

Fig. 2-15

 Use the snap to grid function when possible. Align Blocks to each other. Perfectly vertical and horizontal edges in all the views compile and render faster.

This book is not demonstrating a Sky Box. However, levels should be surrounded by a sky box. **A sky box is a very large hollowed cube with a sky texture (or any other texture) assigned to it.** Your created level sits inside the sky box.

Don't use extremely narrow, elongated, or acute blocks. Always try to design your map with as few surfaces as possible. Gamestudio recommends using thick blocks.

Keep your map small. Blocks render more accurately the closer they are to the center of the map. If you need a large map - use blocks for structures like buildings, and use entities for the details such as columns or posts.

Using Cubes/Blocks to Create Openings between Rooms

1 **Click on OBJECT ➔ ADD CUBE ➔ MEDIUM**. This cube will be placed between the rooms.

2 **Click on the newly created cube. Click on** 🔼 **SCALE** and scale the new cube down to a size that will fit between the two existing rooms.

3 **Click** 🔽 **MOVE** and use the arrow keys/or drag to move the newly created cube between the rooms. Fig. 2-16 shows block being pulled down into position.

4 **ZOOM IN** by moving backwards with the roller on your mouse. Use the right mouse button to move around. Make sure in the Back XZ Grid Screen the new doorway cube is on the room's floor line. Fig. 2-16, 2-17

5 **Position the third cube down into the room to create an opening**
Check multiple views of the block to make sure it is positioned properly.

Cube level with floor.   Fig. 2-16

Third cube highlighted red - positioned between the two main cubes (rooms) ready for CSG Subtract. Be sure to check the cube position in all the views.

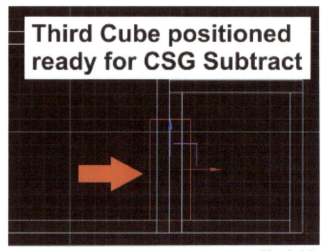

Fig. 2-17

You add CUBES however they appear on the levels tab as "blocks" Only after being Hollowed do the cubes/blocks appear as Groups with blocks under them. A single block on the levels tab is a cube/block that has been added and not hollowed.

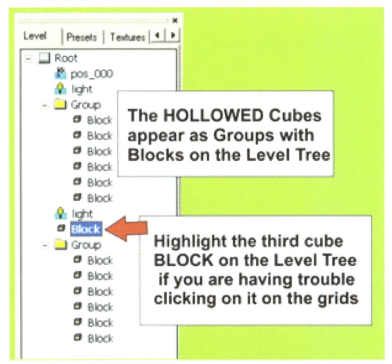

The HOLLOWED Cubes appear as Groups with Blocks on the Level Tree

Highlight the third cube BLOCK on the Level Tree if you are having trouble clicking on it on the grids

Fig. 2-18

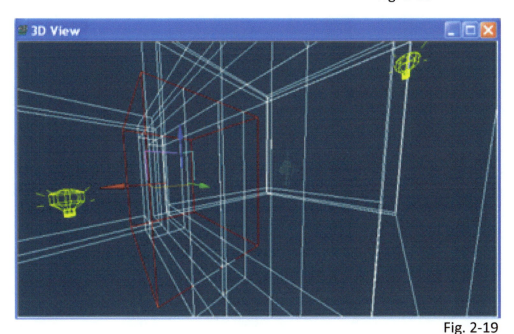

Fig. 2-19

Block (Red) positioned between the two rooms before CSG subtrack

Using Cube/Blocks Blocks to Create Openings between Rooms con't

6   Click EDIT ➔ CSG Subtract. This creates an opening between the two rooms.

7   DELETE the cube/block used to create the opening.

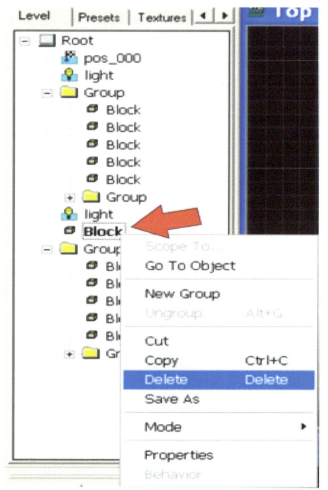

Fig. 2-20

8   FILE ➔ SAVE the Level ➔   Click on BUILD ▦   Click YES to replace with **default texture ➔ Click OK** on Map Compiler ➔ **Click OK to close Map Compiler ➔ Click ▮ RUN ➔ Click OK on Run Level**

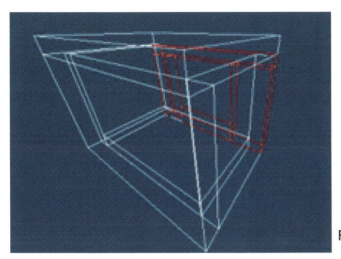

CSG Subtract complete - RED area showing cut-out

Fig 2-21

Finished Rooms with Opening

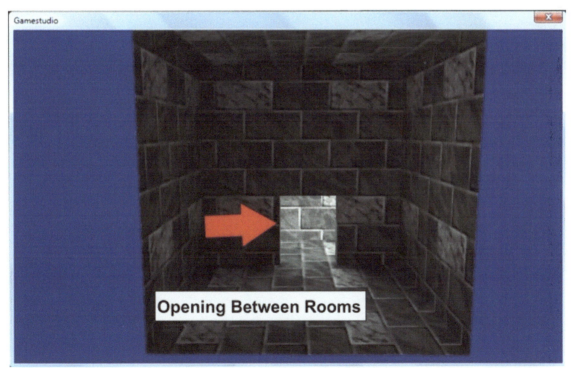

Two rooms connected by opening. Default texture applied.   Fig. 2-22

After Building and Running, the textured finished rooms appear in a separate window.

Chapter 3 - Textures

Fig. 3-1

TEXTURES -are used to make objects look more realistic. You are applying a visual "picture" to the object. **Textures are created in external software programs**, paint.net is the software used in this book.

There are different ways to texture; this book will first show how to **texture the entire block by scoping down into a group**. The selected group first HIGHLIGHTS RED then after clicking **Scope Down** it TURNS WHITE. Select an entire block within the group, such as a roof or wall. The texture will be applied to ALL SIDES of the selected block within that group.

Later, this book will show **how to modify textures and texture each separate surface**. Gamestudio comes with a basic default texture. Other textures are available within the software by opening the standard.wad file under textures.

Opening and Adding "standard.wad" textures

1   On the Textures Tab **Click on DEFAULT.WAD and open it. ➔ Right Click on the DEFAULT. WAD block ➔ Click on Texture Manager. Fig. 3-1**

2   **Click on Add WAD** Fig. 3-2

3   **Click on standard.wad** Fig. 3-3

4   **Click on Open** Fig. 3-3

5 Click OK. At the left of the Grid views under the Textures Tab scroll down to open the standard.wad. Fig. 3-4

Fig. 3-2

Fig. 3-4

Info. Save Textures in the WADS folder.

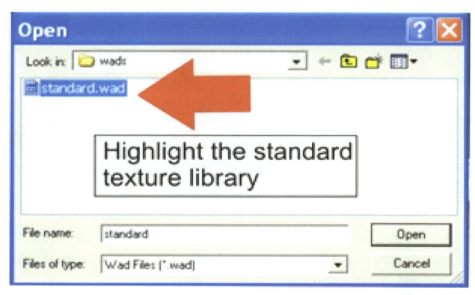

Fig. 3-3

Applying a Texture

1   **Highlight one of the cubes.** This will automatically cause the 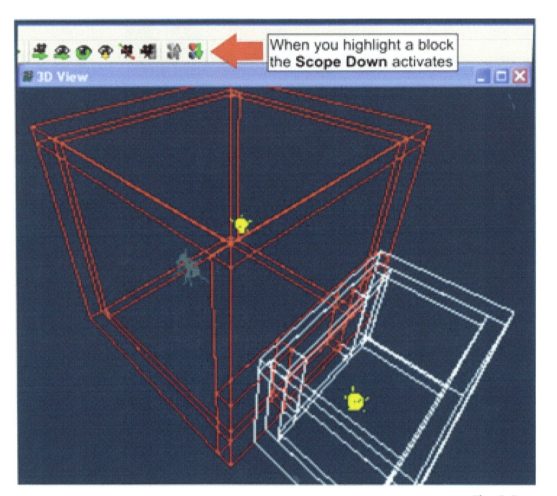 Scope Down to activate and the cube will TURN RED activating the entire cube. Fig. 3-5
TO APPLY THE SAME TEXTURE TO THE ENTIRE CUBE - go to the texture tab and double click on a texture - or Right Click on the texture and Click Apply

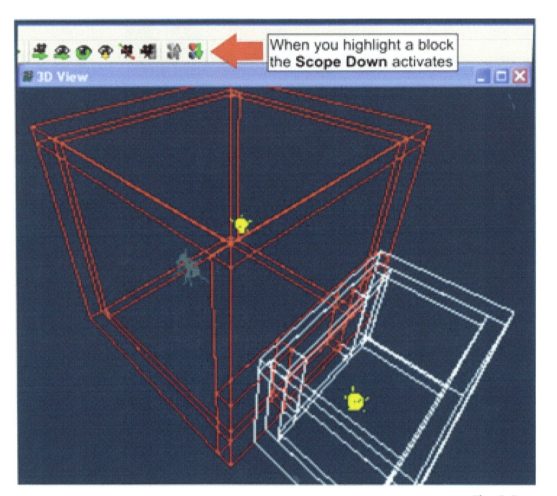

Fig. 3-5

The entire group/cube is selected and ready to be textured or can be scoped down into and texture applied to one block in this group of blocks.

2   Click on **Scope Down.** The cube you selected will CHANGE FROM <u>RED</u> TO <u>WHITE</u>, also only the selected cube will be visable.

3   Click on the ROOF of the Cube. Only the roof block highlights and is ready to be textured. Fig. 3-6
SCROLL DOWN the standard.wad panel to select a texture for the roof.

4   Click on a Texture, ➜ RIGHT CLICK ➜ Click on APPLY.

5   Under View on the Toolbar Click on TEXTURED to view the finished cube with the texture applied. The illustrations have been captured in the WIRE View. Clicking on VIEW on the main menu allows you to switch between the different views to see the cubes in Wire, Solid or Textured views. Fig. 3-7 show the textured view.

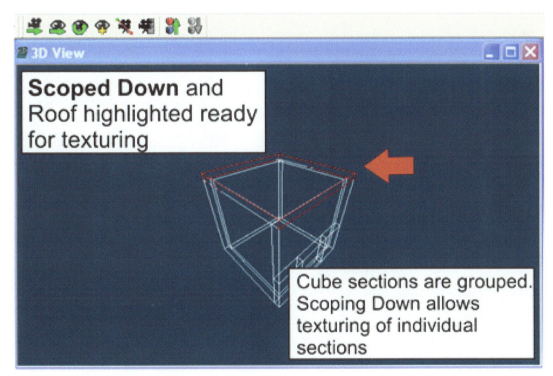

Click on the roof of the cube to start the texturing process.   **Fig. 3-6**
This selects one Block out of the Group. Wire View

6   Click **Scope Up to leave Scope View.**

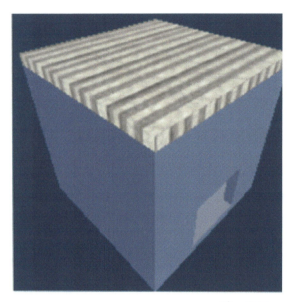

Cube with texture
applied only to the roof.
Textured View

 **Or, add texture by switching back
and forth between the Levels Tab
and the Textures Tab. Figures 3-8
and 3-9**

There are numerous ways to work on
the objects. By switching back and forth
between the Textures Tab and the Levels
Tab you can quickly texture a cube. (group
with blocks) The individual Blocks will be
highlighted under the Levels Tab.

Fig. 3-7

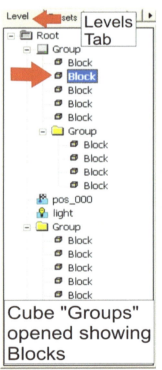

**Go to the
LEVELS TAB
and OPEN all
the GROUPS**
under the Root.
(Fig. 3-8)

**➔ Under
the GROUP
you want to
texture Click
and highlight a
single Block to
texture.**

Fig. 3-8

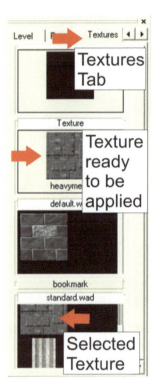

**Switch back to
the TEXTURES
TAB ➔ Double
Click a Texture
to apply to the
selected block.**
(Fig. 3-9)

Double Clicking
is another way to
apply texture.

Fig. 3-9

Bookmark Textures

Open the Bookmarks Panel, Right Click then Click on ADD TEXTURE and the Texture in the Active Texture Panel will be added to the bookmark textures.

Scaling a Texture

In Fig. 3-10 the floor texture pattern is too large for the size of the room.

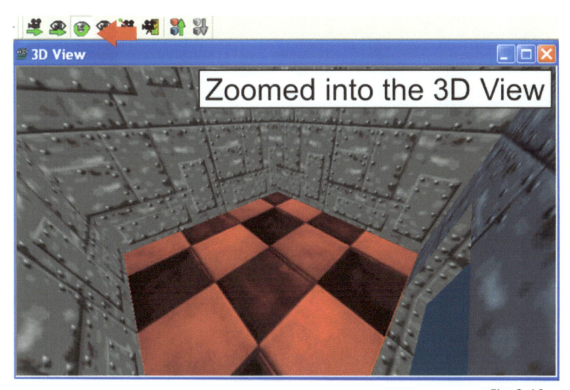

Fig. 3-10

1 **With the floor block highlighted Click on the SURFACE Tab** Fig. 3-11

2 **Lower the X and Y Scales** to make modifications. In this example the X Scale and the Y Scale have been lowered to .2 which decreases the size of the block pattern. Fig. 3-11

3 **Change the ANGLE Scale** to rotate the floor pattern. Fig. 3-11

To highlight a single Block - On the Levels Tab - Select the Group (Cube) then click on each block watching the Views to see which Block highlights - then with that surface highlighted apply a texture. Clicking on the individual blocks on the computer screen view also highlights the block and prepares it for texturing. Later, texturing a Single Surface on a Block will be demonstrated.

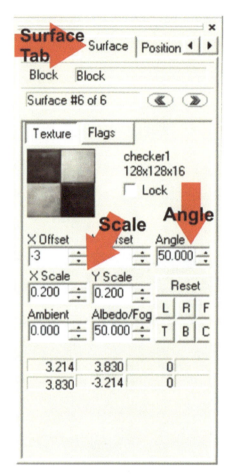

Tile pattern decreased and rotated in the room. Fig. 3-12

Leave the SURFACE settings and apply the floor texture throughout the rooms to obtain a consistent pattern.

By renaming the floor Blocks "floor" in each Group it is easy to click on each floor and apply the same texture and settings throughout the level.

Renaming blocks is covered under - Labeling Groups and Blocks. Page 27

For all non-visible surfaces - bottoms or non-visible sides - mark the **None** flag. Your level will compile faster. It saves texture memory.

The Flags panel selects the attributes of the surface.

Fig. 3-11

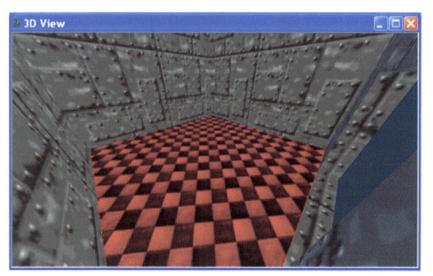

Floor pattern scaled down.

NOTE: The inner floor has been textured with a tile pattern.

The opening between the rooms still has the same texture as the walls.

Fig.3-12

Labeling Groups and Blocks

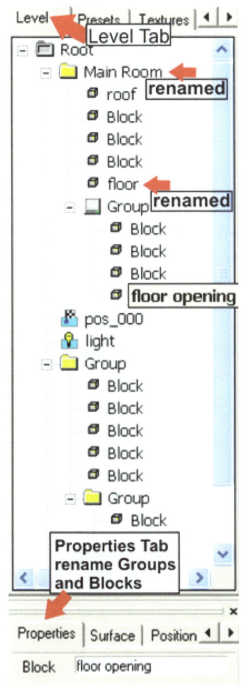

Fig. 3-13

It is easier to texture if each component added to the level is renamed to reflect the environment being created. Ex: Main Room, Passageway, Red Room etc.

1 **Click on a "Group" in the Level Tab beside the folder-** check the 3D View and the other views to be sure the group you have selected is the one you want.

2 **Click on the "Properties Tab"** In the example Fig. 3-13 the Block for the "floor opening" has been changed from the generic "block" to "floor opening".

3 **Click on each "Block" under that Group** and on the **Properties Tab rename the different blocks**.

Default Key Functions

Default functions are attached to the following keys in normal mode and entity viewer mode:

[F2] Quicksave. Saves the game into the file "**save_0.sav**". Can also be used to mark a position in level walkthrough mode.

[F3] Quickload. Loads the last saved game.

[F5] Video resolution up.

[Shift-F5] Video resolution down.

[F6] Takes screenshots to the file "**shot_n. jpg**".

[F12] Toggles music and sound.

[Alt-F4] Shuts down the engine.

[Esc] Shuts down the engine.

[Alt-Enter] Toggles window and fullscreen mode.

from: Conitec - Gamestudio Manual 2010

Default Key Functions can be removed by setting the KEY EVENT function to NULL, or set it to some other function.

Selecting each Block's Separate Surfaces for Texturing

The first example applied texture to all surfaces of the a Block. It is a quick method to texture room surrfaces. The previously example textured a cube's floor with a tile pattern.

To detail the WED environment and apply texture to make objects look more realistic each of the block's sides can be textured separately.

The following example will use the "floor opening" section between the two rooms.

Fig. 3-14 shows the floor section with the same texture on all surfaces of the "floor opening".

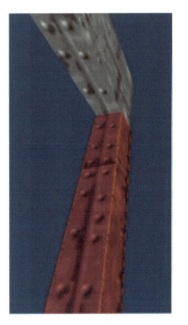

Fig. 3-14

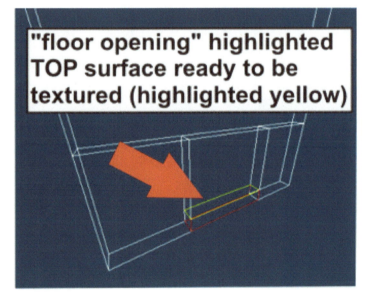

Fig. 3-15

Fig. 3-15 shows the Wire View of the "floor opening".

In **Fig. 3-16** on the Surface Tab the Block "floor opening" shows SURFACE #3 of 6. This is the TOP surface of the "floor opening" block.

It is shown highlighted in **Fig. 3-15**. The Block is highlighted and the active surface ready for texturing is highlighted yellow.

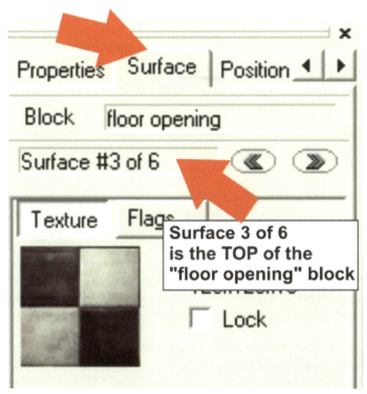

Fig. 3-16

Surface Tab shows Block being textured, what Texture is being applied, and Active Surface (#) number.

Clicking on the Surface Tab will show the current texture and shows the sides of the cubes as numbers 1 of 6, etc.

Click through to view the different surfaces which will be highlighted in yellow.

 SURFACES
"**Shaded** - normal texture with shadow map for static and dynamic lights.
Flat - texture for outside, no shadow map. Flat shaded according to the angle to the sun.
Sky - multilayer sky surface (see manual), necessary for the sky box surrounding the level. Default if the texture name begins with 'sky'.
Turbulence - liquid, warping texture for water or lava. Default if the texture name begins with '*'.
None - surface won't be rendered." *from - Conitec Manual January 2010*

Texturing a Surface

1   **On the LEVELS TAB Double Click on the "floor opening" block or Scope Down into the level and click on the Block you want to texture.** This example is texturing the top floor surface of the opening between the two rooms. (We first highlight the correct BLOCK within the Group.)

2   **Click on the TEXTURES TAB –** select the floor texture to load it into the Texture window. Our example is the black and white tile texture. (Texture window is the top window displaying a sample of the texture under the texture tab.)

3   **Click on the SURFACE TAB – rotate through the surface numbers till the TOP surface is shown as YELLOW in the highlighted Block in the 3D View** (3 of 6)**– Wire View.**

4   **Double Click on the highlighted SURFACE on the View Window to apply the texture - or - RIGHT CLICK on the Texture window under the Texture Tab (you have previously loaded the texture you want to apply into this texture window) Click apply and texture surface 3 of 6 on the "floor opening".** Fig. 3-17

5   **Click on VIEW on the Toolbar and change the View to Textured View**. The 3D window should look like Fig. 3-18 when you zoom into the room in the 3D View. Fig. 3-18 shows the two rooms floors textured and the floor surface of the opening also textured. They all blend together as one floor pattern.

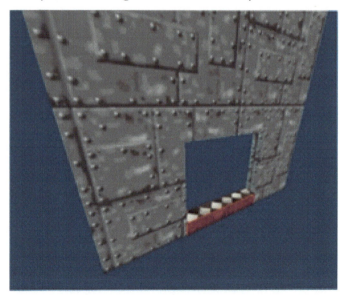

Floor texture applied to only the TOP   Fig. 3-17
SURFACE of the block.

Fig. 3-18 shows the Main Room, the "floor opening" and the additional   Fig. 3-18
room all textured with the same checkered floor pattern. (Walls of the
additional room have not yet been textured. In this example the entire
additional room is highlight.

Info. **TEXTURE COMMANDS:**

Add Texture - adds a PCS, BMP or TGA texture to the WAD.

Apply – applies the texture in the textures window to all the faces of the selected
object. You can also apply the texture by "double clicking" on the selected texture.

Texture Lock – locks a texture to an object if you move it.

Rename – renames the currently selected texture.

Remove – Moves the texture from the WAD.

Add to Bookmarks – adds a texture to your bookmarks.

Save WAD – Saves the WAD file.

Downloading Texture Files from the Internet

1 **Create a folder on your desktop and name it "Textures."**

2 **Download Texture files** from http://au.conitec.net.

3 **Extract the Downloaded Files to your "Textures folder".**
The zipped files will make their own folder in your textures folder.

4 **Next navigate to the Gamestudio installation folder. Start ➔ My Computer ➔Local Drive (C:) ➔ Program Files➔ Gstudio7 ➔ WADS.**

5 **Place the downloaded textures from the desktop folder "Textures" into this WADS folder.**

 Save custom and downloaded textures in the Gstudio7/ WADS folder.

 Additional Textures cannot be added until the standard.wad textures are installed-page 20.

Creating a Folder for your Custom Textures

The next topic discusses using Paint.net. After creating custom textures they can be placed into the standards.wad file or they could be placed into a separate folder "custom textures". the following instructions show how to create a folder for the custom textures within the GStudio WAD folder.

1 **NAVIGATE to Program Files ➔ GStudio7 ➔ WAD**

2 **OPEN the WAD folder**

3 **CREATE a NEW FOLDER named "custom_textures"** This new folder will hold your custom textures.

Paint.net – Creating a Custom Texture

1 OPEN paint.net software ➔Click IMAGE ➔ RESIZE

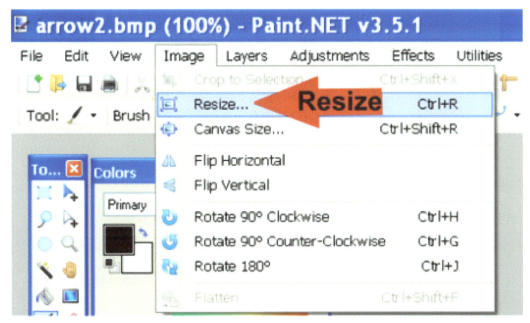

Fig. 3-19

2 Enter 128 x 128 on the Height and Width Pixel Scale ➔ Click OK

3 Create a Custom Texture with Paint.net or Import artwork for your custom texture onto the 128 x 128 canvas. Fig. 3-20
This example is using the custom texture of an orange arrow on a green background. Fig. 3-21

4 SAVE the custom texture in the "custom textures" folder you created in Gstudio7/WAD/custom_textures (page 32) **as either a .TGA, .PCX, .DDS or .BMP format.** The example used is an arrow texture. It is saved as a .TGA. It is a Sprite. Sprites will be discussed in Chapter 5.

Fig. 3-20

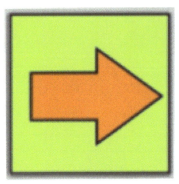

Fig. 3-21

 Images imported into 3D gamestudio have to be a Power of 2 - example; 2 pixel, 4 pixel, 8 pixel etc. Images can be no larger than 1024 x 1024.

 Texture names must use normal letters, digits and underscore. Do not use spaces or special characters. If a texture name begins with a "+" sign followed by a digit the texture will be animated and cycle between "+0... and up to +9". If the texture name begins with "*" the texture will be a passable turbulence texture. Sky textures begin with "sky".

Adding A Custom Texture to the Textures Library in 3D gamestudio

1 **RIGHT CLICK on the "standard.wad" under the Textures Tab**. Fig. 3-22

2 **Click on ADD TEXTURE**

3 **In the Window that opens NAVIGATE to GStudio7/WAD/custom_textures.** Fig. 3-23

4 **OPEN the "custom_textures" folder**

5 **SELECT your custom texture ➔ CLICK OPEN** Fig. 3-23

Fig. 3-22

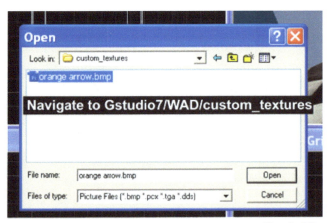

Opening the orange arrow.bmp file. The custom texture will appear in the standard.wad file.   Fig. 3-23

Applying the Custom Texture

1 **On the LEVELS TAB open the GROUP with the arrow wall** (Fig. 3-24) A Block has been labeled "arrow wall" because that is the wall the "custom texture of an arrow will be applied to. (Refer to page 27 for labeling Groups and Blocks)

2 **Click and highlight the "arrow wall" BLOCK.** Fig. 3-24

3 **With the "arrow wall" Block highlighted ➔ GO to the SURFACE TAB** (Bottom of Fig. 3-24) **and rotate through the "surfaces of the 'arrow wall' block" until the Inside Wall is highlighted and ready for a texture.**

4 **On the TEXTURE TAB either Double Click on the Custom Texture or Right Click on the Custom Texture and Click Apply**. Fig. 3-25

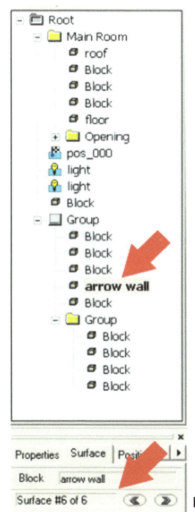

Fig. 3-24

Fig. 3-25

Getting Started with Conitec's 3D Gamestudio   **35**

Another way to apply this texture is to use the Scope Down and Click on the "arrow wall Block" to highlight it , then use the Surface Tab to rotate through the surfaces of the "arrow wall Block" to ONLY highlight the inside wall of the second room. Then apply the texture.

In this **first example** our custom texture will be applied to the entire wall of the second room.

The **second example** will create a new cube and apply the custom texture to that small cube which will be attached to the wall and hang like a painting.

Adjusting Textures on the X Scale and Y Scale

After applying the custom texture, fig. 3-26 shows that it is not positioned properly on the wall.

Fig. 3-26

With the "arrow wall" highlighted make adjustments on the SURFACE TAB on the X Scale and the Y Scale until the texture is lined up properly. Fig. 3-27

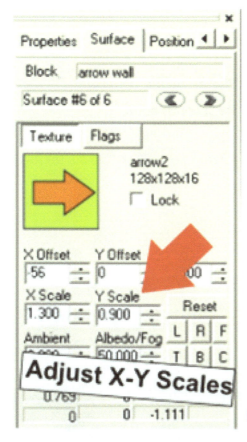

Fig. 3-27

X and Y Scales

Use the adjustment keys on the X Scale and the Y Scale to adjust the applied texture.

A straight pattern like the arrow will not require any adjustments on the Angle.

The tile floor in Fig. 3-26 and Fig. 3-28 was previously scaled down and it was also angled.

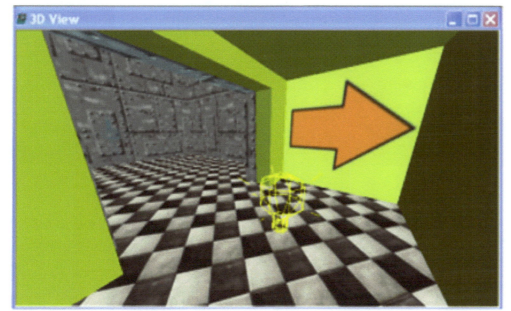

Fig. 3-28

Adding Textures – Other Techniques

1   **Click OBJECT Add Cube - small**

2   **SCALE the cube down to the size of a picture on a wall, thin rectangle.**

3   **Line up the cube/Block to the Inside Wall of the second room.**
     The lines should touch. Do not hollow the Block.

4   **With the Cube/Block highlighted apply your custom texture ex: "arrow texture".**

5   **Make adjustments on the X Scale and Y Scale.**

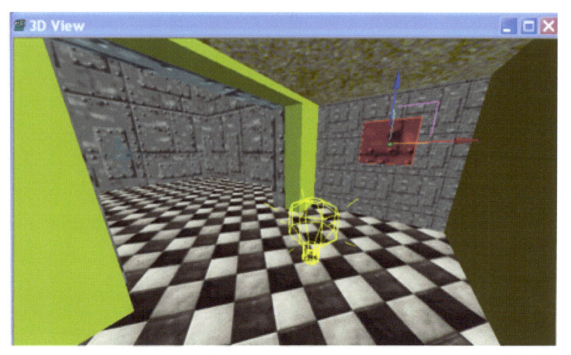

Fig. 3-29

This small cube is not hollowed. The cube is simply used as a picture frame to hold the arrow texture. Scale the cube down and make it narrow (thin) to hang on the wall. Place the inner wall surface against the outer surface of the small cube. Highlight the small cube and apply the custom texture.

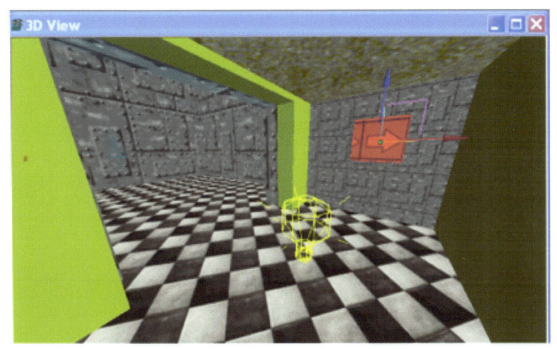

Custom texture is not properly adjusted.   Fig. 3-30

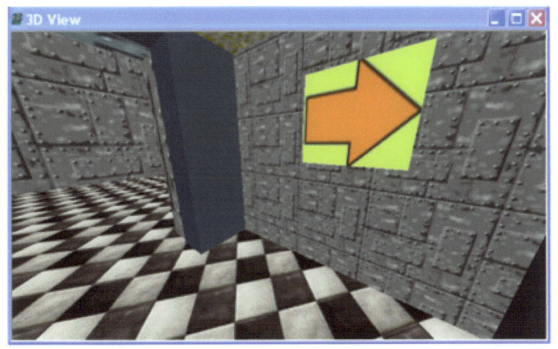

Properly adjusted texture   Fig. 3-31

Chapter 4 – Primitives

3D graphic elements are created from points, lines and triangles. 3D model files contain vertex information which includes among other things the X, Y and Z positions. A 3D object consists of 3D points, X, Y, and Z.

Primitive objects are designed in space using the Cartesian coordinate system and positions are mapped in the X, Y, and Z planes. The center of the 3D graphics world is (0, 0, 0) the **origin**. The X, Y and Z coordinates determine where in space the game objects are positioned.

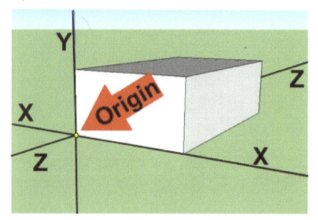

Fig. 4-1

Primitives are non-animated. Primitives are 3-dimensional shapes.

Gamestudio primitives are computer graphic elements which are used as building blocks.

The basic concept of Gamestudio's design is the use of Object Oriented editing. Users design and create using Gamestudio's primary elements. Users piece together simple forms to create more complex forms.

These forms or objects are created from Primitives. Primitives are by definition "the basic, original, or at the beginning." There are three primary elements in the Gamestudio level; blocks, terrain and entities. **Gamestudio defines their blocks as "a solid, non-animated textured object in any shape."** These blocks are shown on the screen in the four grids; **Top** (XY) Grid, **Back** (XZ) Grid, **Side** (YZ) Grid and the **3D View**.

Gamestudio Primitives   Fig. 4-2

The software also has an extensive list of **PreFabs** on the menu bar under OBJECT such as; arches, bridges, buildings, furniture, etc. Users have the option of importing primitives from outside 3D libraries. See the Help Menu within Gamestudio's software for information about importing files.

Gamestudio's Primitives

Gamestudio provides several **primitives.** At the time this book was written they were; Cylinders, Pyramids, Lumber, Spheres and a miscellaneous group of primitives; House, Plate (small), Plate (large), Tent and Trapezoid.

These primitives are found under **OBJECT ➜ ADD PRIMITIVE.**

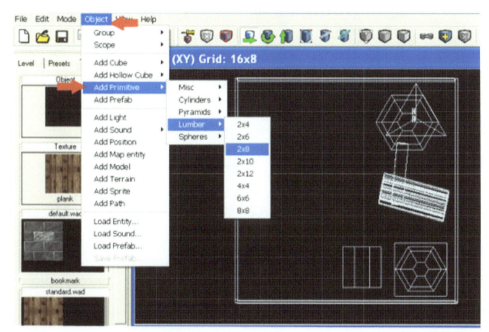

Fig. 4-3

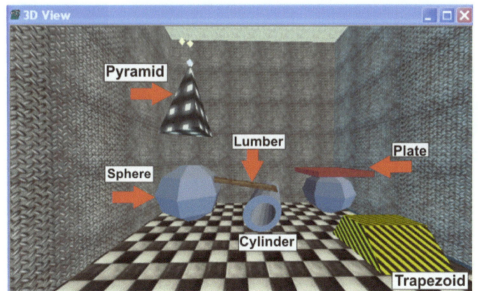

NOTE: The Cylinder has been hollowed out. Cylinders are normally solid.

Fig. 4-4

Creating a Light with Primitives

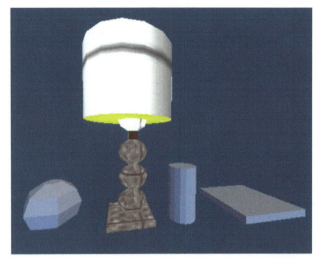

This example will show how to create a structure in the WED level editor using the basic primitive shapes without any background. Start a folder of the structures you create, like this lamp, and save each structure to this folder.

Textures used for this lamp are from the standard.wad folder in the Gamestudio WED software.

This lamp is a complex structure that is made from three primitives; a sphere, a cylinder and a plate.

Fig. 4-5

1   **FILE ➔   NEW LEVEL ➔   Click OBJECT ➔ ADD PRIMITIVE ➔ MISC ➔ PLATE SMALL.**

2   **Click on the Plate and Resize the plate using the arrows with the Scale Command activated.** (Base of the lamp)

3   **Click OBJECT ➔ ADD PRIMITIVE ➔ SPHERE ➔ 26 SIDED.**

4   **Click on the sphere and Resize the sphere using the arrows with the Scale Command activated.**

5   **Click on the sphere ➔** (DUPLICATE the sphere 3 times) **Hold the Control Key while hitting the "D" key 3 times.**

6   **Place three (3) of the Spheres on top of each other using the Plate as the bottom "base." With the** Move Command activated – match surfaces by zooming in fully and making adjustments (check all three Grid views).

7   **Place the extra sphere over to the side for later use.**

8   **Click OBJECT ➔ ADD PRIMITIVE ➔CYLINDER ➔ 16 SIDED.**

9   **Resize the Cylinder with the Scale** Command activated. (small cylinder for base of light bulb) Fig. 4-6

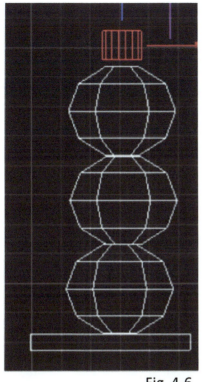

Fig. 4-6

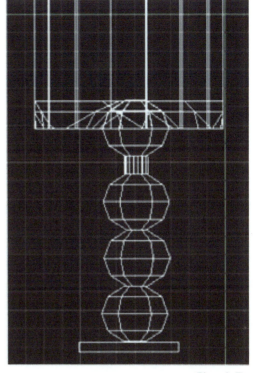

Fig. 4-7

10 Place the small cylinder on the top sphere with the Move Command activated. Fig. 4-6

11 With the Move Command activated pull the extra sphere over and align it on top of the small cylinder (this sphere is the light bulb). Fig. 4-7

12 Click OBJECT ➔ ADD PRIMITIVE ➔ CYLINDER ➔ 16 SIDED.

13 Resize the Cylinder with the Scale Command activated to create a lampshade.

14 Place the lampshade Cylinder half way down over the top "light bulb" Sphere. Fig. 4-7

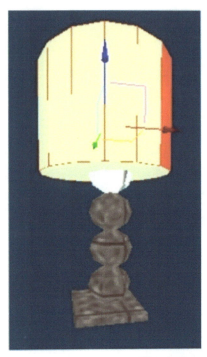

Fig. 4-8

15 Texture the individual primitives.

Refer to Section 2 for texturing.

The texturing used was changed under the Surface Tab; angles were changed and the X Scale & Y Scale reduced or increased for the separate primitives.

The lampshade texture was manipulated to bring the dark outer band on the existing texture down to form the line around the top portion of the lampshade.

Each block surface in the lampshade can also be changed with the same texture and manipulated on the X Scale and Y Scale, along with adjustments to the Angle under the Surface Tab to create shading effects.

15 Click on the top "light bulb" sphere → Control "D" Duplicate the top sphere.

16 MOVE the duplicate sphere over to the side and texture it. Fig. 4-9

17 Highlight the top "light bulb" sphere which is halfway under the "lampshade" Cylinder. Fig. 4-10

18 Click EDIT → CSG Subtract.

19 The light bulb sphere will "take out – subtract" a portion of the lampshade cylinder.

20 With the light bulb sphere still highlighted DELETE it. Fig. 4-11

21 The subtracted section of the lampshade cylinder will be visible.

22 Pull the duplicate "light bulb" sphere over and position it in the same exact location of the original light bulb. Fig. 4-11

23 Highlight all the primitives in the structure by Clicking on the Left Mouse Button and Pulling and Dragging a Box around the entire lamp structure. Fig. 4-12

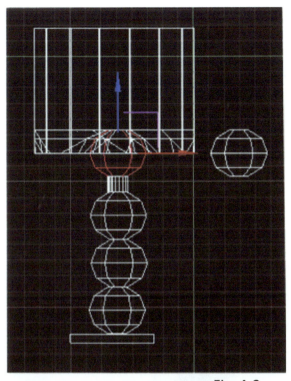

Fig. 4-9

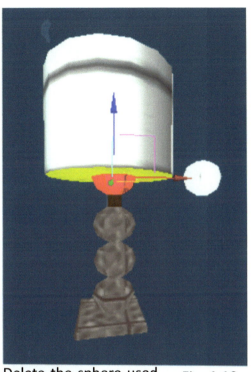

Delete the sphere used for CSG Stract

Fig. 4-10

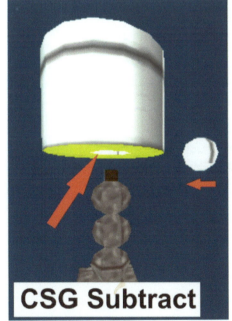

CSG Subtract

Slide duplicate sphere under lampshade.

Fig. 4-11

Fig. 4-12

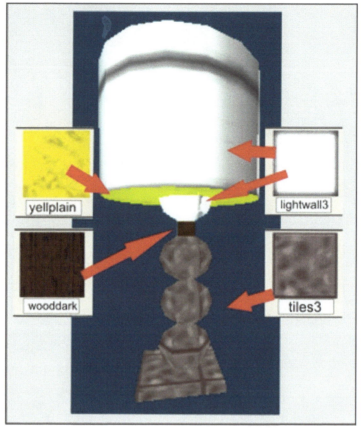

Finished lamp   Fig. 4-13

24   Click OBJECT ➔ GROUP ➔ GROUP TOGETHER or (Ctrl+G) Fig. 4-12

25   Save as .WMP file extension

26   The standard lighting is dim when viewing the structure without a room background. ADD a Light Click OBJECT ➔ ADD LIGHT and position a few lights around the structure.

27 Click BUILD

28 Click RUN

A separate window appears showing the compiled file.

PROBLEMS: Sometimes the **Run Level** adds extra characters at the end of the file extension and this prevents the file from running properly. To correct this, ERASE the Extra Characters after the .wmb before hitting OK on the Run Level. First try running the level and if the level won't run try this fix.

Fig. 4-14

Editing a Primitive

It is possible to edit the **PreFabs** which come with the Gamestudio WED software. This example will change the steps on a flight of stairs in the PreFab library.

1   FILE ➔ NEW LEVEL ➔ OBJECT ➔ PreFab ➔ UPSTAIRS ➔ WINDIN02 ➔ OK

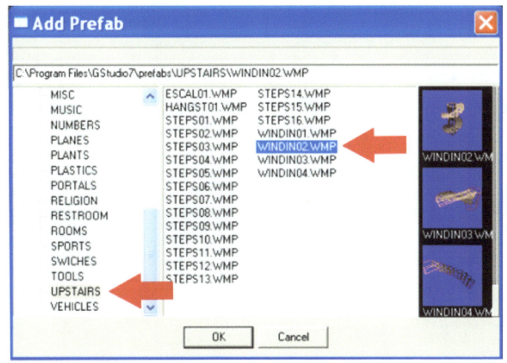

Fig. 4-15

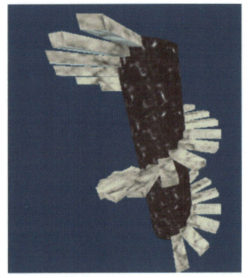

PreFab WINDIN02   Fig. 4-16

Fig. 4-17

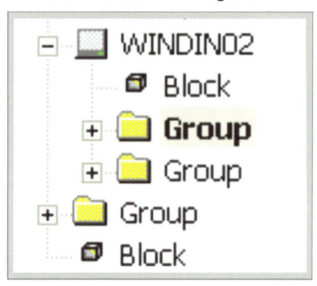

Levels Tab - First Group Folder under   Fig. 4-18
WINDIN02 - upper portion of stairs

2   **Click on the LEVELS TAB ➔ CLICK ON WINDIN02 FOLDER ➔CLICK ON THE FIRST GROUP FOLDER** . This will highlight the top portion of the steps. This process will texture all sides of the steps with the same texture. Opening the Group Folder will allow texturing each step separately. This example is texturing all the steps the same. Fig. 4-18

3   **Click on the TEXTURES TAB ➔ in the standard.wad folder choose a different color for the steps on the spiral stairway ➔ RIGHT CLICK ➔ APPLY** This example is applying a wooden texture to the steps. Fig. 4-17

4   **Repeat for the second group folder,** which is the lower stairs. Fig. 4-17 Lower portion of stairs highlighted and ready for wooden texture.

5   **FILE ➔ SAVE .wmp file extension**

Adding an Upper Level & Adding Stairs

To create an upper level start with two cubes re-sized and placed one on top of the other. Cut out an opening in the roof of the lower level and the floor of the upper level and place a stairway in the opening. Directions below give step by step instructions but do not include illustrations of all the steps involved. Refer back to previous sections for creating rooms, CSG Subtract, Texturing, etc.

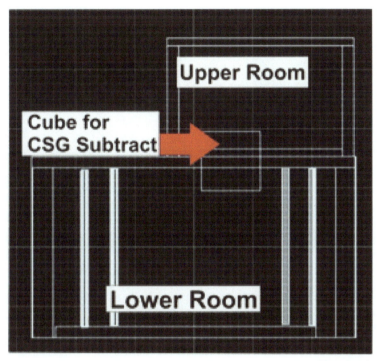

Fig. 4-19

1   FILE →NEW LEVEL →OBJECT → ADD CUBE → Large

2   With MOVE   activated RESIZE the Cube →EDIT → Hollow Block

3   OBJECT → ADD CUBE → Large (this is the second cube for the top floor)

4   With MOVE   activated RESIZE the Cube

5   EDIT → Hollow Block

6   Position the Upper Room Cube on top of the Lower Room touching outer lines.

7   OBJECT ➔ ADD CUBE ➔Small (This cube will only be used for CSG Subtract)

8   Position the Small Un-Hollowed Cube between the two rooms. Fig. 4-20

9   EDIT ➔ CSG Subtract ➔ DELETE the Cube

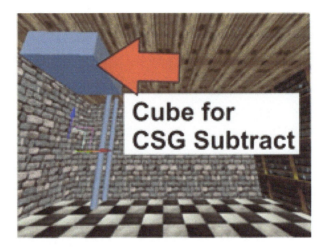

Fig. 4-20

10 Apply Texture to the surfaces of the Upper and Lower Rooms
    (Refer to Section 2 Textures)

11 Add Stairs - OBJECT ➔ PreFab ➔ UPSTAIRS ➔ WINDIN02 (or add the re-textured
    stairs from the previous lesson Fig. 4-17) (Fig. 4-22 Finished Room with stairs)

12 This example has four columns created by adding OBJECT ➔ ADD PRIMITIVE ➔
    CYLINDER ➔ 16 SIDED. The Cylinders are positioned parallel to the winding stairs.

13 Save As

14 BUILD  ➔ RUN

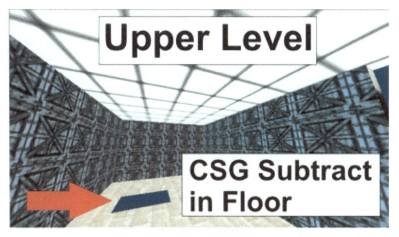

Fig. 4-21

Fig. 4-22

Finished project with a main room, stairs leading to an upstairs room. The stairs were the PreFab stairs from the section on Editing A Primitive. The poles were cylinders with metal texture applied from the standards.wad folder. Stairs were positioned in the opening leading to the upstairs.

Chapter 5 – Entities

Gamestudio's engine supports the following ENTITIES; Models, Sprites, Sublevels (Map Entities) **and Terrain** (Unchunked and Chunked).

Entities can be created with script, or in WED. They are external files read from the path or work folder.

MODELS are animated 3D objects. They are stored in an external MDL file. Models have a 3D mesh with skeleton bones and skin. They are used as moveable or animated objects and they can cast dynamic shadows. Models are WMBs in Gamestudio's Map Entity extension.

SPRITES (Billboards) are flat 2D objects. They are stored in external PCX, BMP, TGA & DDS files, and they can be created in paint programs such as; Paint.net, Photoshop, etc. Sprites can contain an alpha channel which has a transparency value for the pixels. Earlier in this book the Arrow texture in the textures section was created and saved as a .TGA file using the Paint.net software. It was a sprite. Sprites act as Decals, they can be placed on floors or walls and they stand upright in landscapes like a billboard. If a sprite's angles are zero it stands upright and will horizontally face the camera. Four sprites can be placed as an "X" shape and create plants or trees. Set the Pan and Tilt at "0" and the roll angle at nonzero the sprite will face the camera in two directions. Animated sprites use PCS, BMP and TGA formats, the DDS format will not support animation.

SUBLEVELS (Map Entities) are small compiled levels stored in an external .WMP file format. They are compiled maps and can be used in the levels as moving doors, platforms, or vehicles. They can be created in WED. PreFabs can be converted into Map Entities by loading the PreFab as a Map and Building the Map Entity then copying it as a .WMB file and placing it in the current level directory.

TERRAIN is one or more textures mapped onto a rectangular grid of height values. They can be created with MED, imported from RAW height maps, or can be built with terrain builder programs and import BMP, PCX height image bitmaps. Passable terrains such as water allow characters in a game to wade, swim or dive. The engine supports unchunked and chunked terrain. Chunked terrain allows faster terrain rendering.

Downloading Models from the Gamestudio's website

 Version 7 of Conitec's Gamestudio does not have models in the WED. Models are available at Conitec's website. The following instructions are for downloading the Gamestudio 7 models, if you have a paid version of the software

1   **Go to** http://www.gamestudio.com

Fig. 5 - 1

2   **Click on DOWNLOAD**

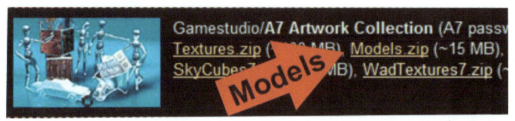

Fig. 5 -2

3   **At the Gamestudio Downloads Page under Software & Tutorials SCROLL DOWN to Gamestuio A7 Artwork Collection (A7 password required)**

4   **Click on Models.zip ➜ Authentication Required opens. Fig. 5-3**

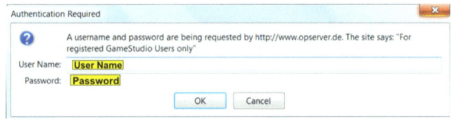

Fig. 5 -3

5   **FIND YOUR USER NAME – PASSWORD by looking in the WED, Click on HELP →
Click on About WED. Fig. 5-4**

6   **About WED opens – GET User ID and Password to use on Gamestudio Site to
download Models. Fig. 5-5**

7   **Use the User ID and Password from the WED About Help Window and enter
them into the Authentication Required Window at Gamestudio's Download Page.
Click OK (Fig. 5-5 Your ID, Password, Fig. 5-3 Enter your ID, Password)**

8   **Unzip the Models folder which has been downloaded. Place the unzipped folder
containing the model files into the directory where 3D GameStudio was installed.
(C:\Program Files\GStudio7)**

9   **To bring a Model into the Gamestudio WED level Click OBJECT → Load Entity →
Browse to the Models folder →Click on Actors → Choose an Actor to load into the
level.** Fig. 5-6

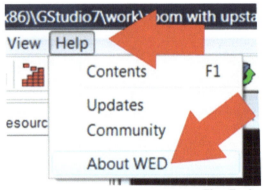

Fig. 5 -4

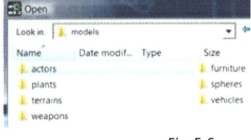

Fig. 5-6

Fig.5 -5

Adding a Computer and Human Player - Starting a Game

This example will cover; opening a level, using the Map Properties, Property Manager, Load Entities (players), and Assigning Behaviors to players in a game.

Design and Create a Level for your game. We are using the "roomwithupstairs5" and adding a cubes for the cyberbabe actor to hide behind.

Three cubes were created for the level. One cube is textured with a wood texture. Two other cubes have been created, textured and added to the level. One cube has a bullseye texture. The other cube has the word dangerous on the cube. Both textures were created in the paint.net software, saved to the custom textures folder and added to the standard.wad file .

The first step is to **ADD a SCRIPT.**

Adding a Script

A script is required for the first level of a game. To program a game yourself use "Empty Script." This example will use a Gamestudio **game genre** which uses a predefined template script.

A **Script** is either a program or a sequence of instructions another program interprets and runs. **Template scripts** have functions and artwork used for the interface, effects, player movement, enemies etc. These templates allow users to create games without requiring any programming.

All of the template scripts can be combined and customized for various games. New scripts are available at Gamestudio's website in the template section of the user forum and in the magazine AUM. New scripts can be created using the C-Script program.

To add a Template Script to a game, first create a Game Script in WED.

This example will assume the user has the level created and open.

1   **Click on FILE ➔ SAVE AS** (name your Level without using spaces in the name, this example is roomwithupstairs5.wmp)

2   Click on FILE ➔ BUILD MAP ➔ Click "OK" Fig. 5-7

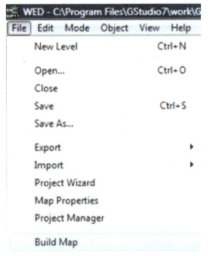

Fig. 5 -7

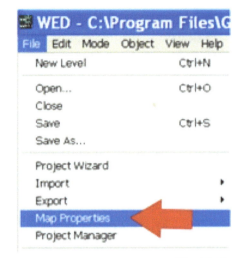

Fig. 5 -8

3   Click FILE ➔ MAP PROPERTIES Fig. 5-8 ➔ **Click on the Folder beside Palette**
Fig. 5-9 (select the file you want to build your game in.
(our example-roomwithupstairs5.wmp)

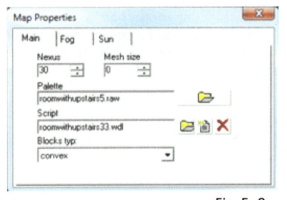

Fig. 5 -9

Fig. 5 -10

4   Click on the file, it appears beside FILE NAME ➔ Click OPEN. The file loads into
the Palette. Fig. 5 -10

5   Next, Click on the **NEW SCRIPT ICON** next to Script. (Fig. 5-11)

Fig. 5-11

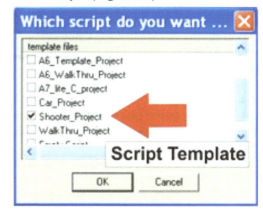

Shooter Project is checked   Fig. 5-12

Fig. 5-13

6   The window "Which Script do you Want to Create" opens. (Fig. 5 -12)

7   Check the type (genre) of game you want to create. We are selecting "Shooter Project" ➔ **Click OK** (Fig. 5-12)

8   The Map Properties Window - the file roomwithupstairs5.wdl is in the SCRIPT box. ➔ **CLOSE THE Map Properties Window** (Fig. 5-13)

Adding Players

9   Click **OBJECT** ➔**LOAD ENTITY** ➔ navigate to the **MODEL FOLDER** you downloaded from Gamestudio's website. (See page 54 number 8)

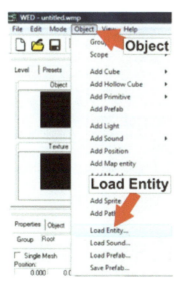

Fig. 5 -14

10 **OPEN the MODELS FOLDER →OPEN the ACTORS FOLDER → Click on human1 → human1 LOADS into File Name → Click on OPEN** (You should see the Human1 actor inside the level, pull the actor down to just above the floor. Do not place actors on the floor they could get stuck onto the floor and not perform their behaviors)

11 **Add a second Actor** (We are loading cyberbabe.) **OBJECT →LOAD ENTITY → ACTORS → cyberbabe →the OPEN Window appears Click on cbabe → cbabe loads into File Name → Click on OPEN** (the second actor is loaded into the level)

Rotate the actors in preparation for action.

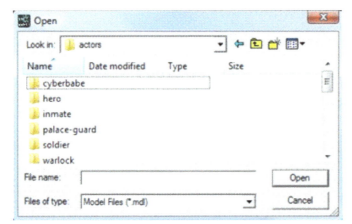

Fig. 5 -15

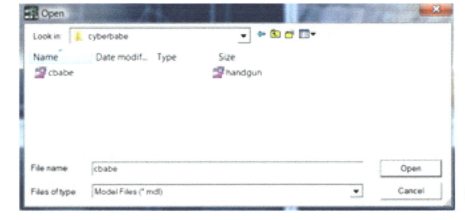

Fig. 5 -16

Fig. 5 -17

Fig. 5 -18

12 Cyberbabe loaded into the level in mid-air. Pull the players down to just above the floor. Placing the players on the floor could cause the players to get stuck in the floor. (Fig. 5-17, 5-18)

13 **SELECT human1** (Click to highlight)

14 **Right Click on the human1 player SELECT BEHAVIOR**. Fig 5-19

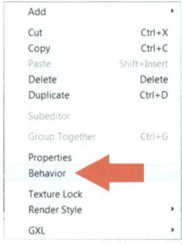

Fig. 5 -19

15 **CHOOSE ACTION Folder opens ➔ SELECT PlBiped01 ➔ Click on OK** (This gives the human actor this action under the behavior tab) Fig. 5-20

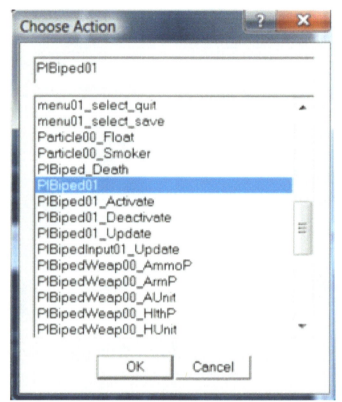

Fig. 5 -20

16 **Highlight cbabe ➔ Click on Behavior Tab ➔ Click on ACTION Folder ➔ "CHOOSE ACTION" Window opens ➔ SELECT AIFPS01_Guard ➔ Click on OK (This is an alternate way of assigning action) FILE ➔ SAVE**

17 **Click on BUILD**

18 **Map Compiler Window opens ➔ Click OK**

19 **Click on RUN ➔ the Run Level Window appears ➔ Click OK**

A Separate Game Window appears.

20 **Press "F5" to increase the size of the game window** – up to 4 increases

Behavior was added to the actors in two different ways; steps 14-15 for the human shows how to add a behavior by right clicking on the actor, and step 16 for cbabe adds the behavior via the Behavior Tab.
In Fig. 5-22 Cbabe was positioned behind the wooden box when the game started. If she can see you she will shoot at you at the start of the game. Start the game with one of the players hiding.

Fig. 5 -21

Fig. 5 -22

Lighting is important. Light highlights certain areas and creates atmosphere.   Fig. 5 -23

Fig. 5-24

Chapter 6 - The Game

Moving Around In The Game

Use the "W" key to move your character forward. (Can you hear the footsteps?)

Use the "S" key to move your character backward.

The "A" key moves left.

The "D" key moves right.

Navigate around the room.

Letters "Q" and "E" pressed simultaneously start your weapon.

Letters "Q" and "E" pressed simultaneously change the weapon.

Click the LEFT MOUSE BUTTON to fire the weapon.

Press letters "Q" and "E" simultaneously to start your weapon ➔ weapon appears on the screen in front of you ➔ Aim the weapon using the crosshair on the screen ➔ to Change the weapon press "Q" and "E" simultaneously ➔ Walk forward toward the cyberbabe, she will automatically fire her weapon at you. She walks toward you when you get within a certain distance.

Fig. 6 - 1

Chapter 7 - Project Manager

Project Manager

The **Project Manager** builds a game project from predefined, customizable **Template Scripts**.

Template Scripts can be combined and customized for unique requirements in your game.

Adding a Script - Page 55 covers this topic.

 Before the **Project Manager** can be used -

First create the **game script**.

To add a **Template Script** - create a **Game Script** in WED

FILE ➔ MAP PROPERTIES ➔ SCRIPT ➔ NEW

The requester window appears - Select the Game Genre

After the Game Script has been added, changes can be made in the Project Manager.

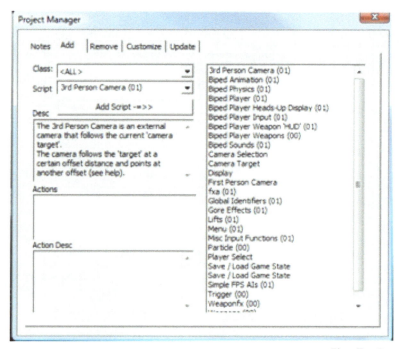

Fig. 7 - 1

Chapter 8 - Publishing A Game

Publishing A Game

Games created with Gamestudio can run on Windows Computers. To publish your game **Click on FILE ➔ PUBLISH** (have Compile EXE checked).

Do not use any spaces or different keyboard characters (dashes symbols etc.) in the game name.

The published game will be created in its own folder within the Gamestudio WORK Folder. All of the files within this folder are needed to run and distribute the game.

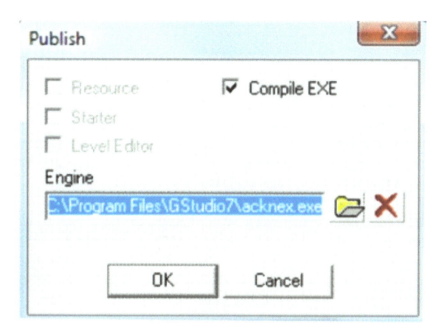

Fig. 8 - 1

Complete information about publishing your game can be found at this location: http://www.conitec.net/beta/acknex.htm

Chapter 9 - Designing A Game Project

Designing A Game Project

The first step is to have a goal. What will the game player do, experience, learn, create, master? What is the purpose of the game? Will the player be a single person inside the game trying to achieve a goal with a time limit? Will the game be a first person shooter game, real-time strategy game, role playing, action game, card game, tile game, puzzle game, word game, or a multi-player environment with the goal of mastering levels within the game? First, decide on the goal of the game.

Then, design an environment for the game. Take time to draw out the environment with paper and pencil as a guide while creating the environment with the software. What characters will be used in the game? Is the game a fantasy world with robots that have human abilities?

Don't have the game players so involved in interacting with the environment or other players that it becomes boring or almost impossible to achieve the objective of the game. Games should be fun and to a certain extent be unpredictable. However, if you are designing an educational game with learning levels such as vocabulary words or geographic places that must be mastered before moving on in the game, then a predictable straight line sequence is appropriate.

Will this game be for personal use or will it be marketed and sold? Creating a commercial game requires level design, script programming, modeling, and shader programming. There are many examples of people who have successfully marketed their games. Gamestudio software has been used to design a variety of games. The most sophisticated game created to date with the software has been "3D Driving Academy." The game with the most distributable copies is , "Great Clips Racing". To find other examples and read short definitions of 3D game Terminology visit:
http://www.conitec.com/english/gstudio/faq.php

Go to Conitec's website and read about the features offered in the four editions of 3D gamestudio:
http://www.conitec.net/english/gstudio/order7.php
Whether you want to develop a classical game or a more sophisticated game, gamestudio has a version to help you develop your project.

Visual Index

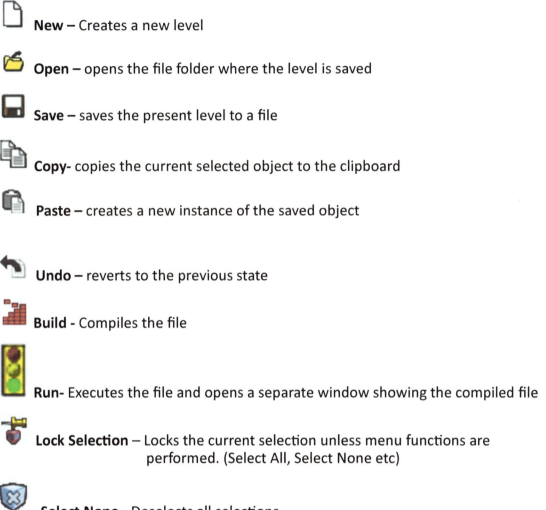

New – Creates a new level

Open – opens the file folder where the level is saved

Save – saves the present level to a file

Copy- copies the current selected object to the clipboard

Paste – creates a new instance of the saved object

Undo – reverts to the previous state

Build - Compiles the file

Run- Executes the file and opens a separate window showing the compiled file

Lock Selection – Locks the current selection unless menu functions are performed. (Select All, Select None etc)

Select None - Deselects all selections

Select – Create a box around an object, or click on the object. To select several objects create a box around all the objects.

Move - Move the current selection

Rotate – Rotate selected object/objects
up/down to rotate clockwise/counterclockwise.
vertically dragging arrow rotates about the arrow axis. NOTE do not rotate terrain.

 **Snap value** –faces & vertices rotate in set snap increments. Snap value determine precision of the rotation. Lower numbers give more precision, higher numbers make aligning objects   easier. Uncheck to rotate manually. NOTE do not rotate terrain.

 Scale - current selection, Hold Control while Scaling to SCALE
Proportionately

 Edit Box – scales, rotates and moves the selected object. Pull on white nodes to control object.

 Slice Wire – Cut the selected object with a wire, press ENTER to cut.

 Slice Plane – Cut the selected object with a plane, press ENTER to cut. The Slice Plane cuts an entire group along a plane.

 Vertex Move – Move a vertex of the selected object. Applies to blocks or paths. Modify the shape of a block.

 Edge Move - Move an edge on the selected object.

 Face Move – Move a face on the selected object.

 Mirror – Mirrors the current selection on the Axis.

 Add Object – Add new object.

Delete Object – Delete the selected object.

 **Grid Scale**

Camera Move If curser is on a object the object wil spin around a center point.

Move Eye Changes the position of where the virtual "eye" is looking in the editing windows

Rotate Eye Changes the orientation of the view in the 3D edit window

Zoom Eye 3D view, increases and descreases distance between the 3D view's "eye" position and editing focus point.

Camera Position - Use to rotate the oject in 3D View. Set a point (green) and use the red point to move an object around the first set point.

Walk-Thru Use the mouse to look left, right, up and down- Move using the Arrow keys or the right mouse button. Pressing [Shift] doubles the speed. [Home] and [End] will move you vertically. [PgUp], [PgDn], and Left / Right let you turn about your main axes. Press [ESC], [SpaceBar], or the [Enter] key at any time to quit out of the Walkthrough Mode.

Scope Up / Scope Down - Scope Down "enter" the view, Scope Up "exits". When activated other objects disappear and only the scoped object is visible.

INDEX

Symbols

www.ingramcontent.com/pod-product-compliance
Lightning Source LLC
Chambersburg PA
CBHW050937060326
40689CB00040B/604